The Soldier's Life in the Civil War

Untold History of the Civil War

CHELSEA HOUSE PUBLISHERS

Untold History of the Civil War

The Soldier's Life in the Civil War

Douglas J. Savage

CHELSEA HOUSE PUBLISHERS
Philadelphia

Produced by Combined Publishing
P.O. Box 307, Conshohocken, Pennsylvania 19428
1-800-418-6065
E-mail:combined@combinedpublishing.com
web:www.combinedpublishing.com

CHELSEA HOUSE PUBLISHERS

Editor in Chief: Stephen Reginald
Managing Editor: James D. Gallagher
Production Manager: Pamela Loos
Art Director: Sara Davis
Director of Photography: Judy L. Hasday
Senior Production Editor: LeeAnne Gelletly
Assistant Editor: Anne Hill

Front Cover Illustration: "The Outpost" by Keith Rocco. Courtesy of
        Tradition Studios ©Keith Rocco

The Chelsea House World Wide Web site address is
http://www.chelseahouse.com

First Printing

135798642

Library of Congress Cataloging-in-Publication Data applied for:
ISBN 0-7910-5710-0

Contents

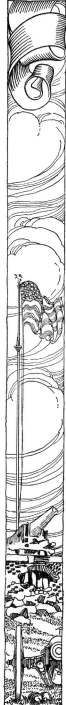

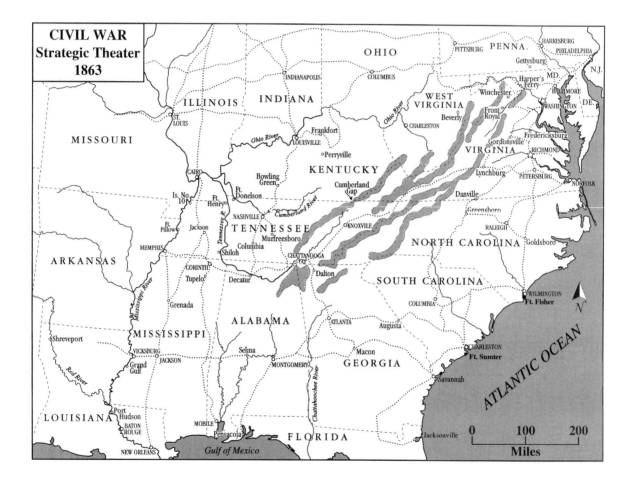

CIVIL WAR
Strategic Theater
1863

OHIO

PENNA.

HARRISBURG

PITTSBURG

Gettysburg

PHILADELPHIA

MD.

N.J.

INDIANAPOLIS

COLUMBUS

WEST
VIRGINIA

Winchester

Harper's
Ferry

BALTIMORE

DE.

ILLINOIS

INDIANA

Beverly

Front
Royal

WASHINGTON

Ohio River

St.
LOUIS

Ohio River

Frankfort

LOUISVILLE

Perryville

CHARLESTON

Gordonsville

Fredericksburg

VIRGINIA

RICHMOND

MISSOURI

CAIRO

KENTUCKY

Cumberland
Gap

Lynchburg

PETERSBURG

NORFOLK

Is. No.
10

Ft.
Henry

Ft.
Donelson

Bowling
Green

Cumberland River

Danville

Greensboro

NASHVILLE

KNOXVILLE

RALEIGH

Goldsboro

Ft.
Pillow

Jackson

TENNESSEE

Murfreesboro

Tennessee River

Columbia

NORTH CAROLINA

MEMPHIS

Shiloh

CHATTANOOGA

CORINTH

Dalton

SOUTH CAROLINA

ARKANSAS

Tupelo

Decatur

Mississippi River

Grenada

ALABAMA

ATLANTA

Augusta

COLUMBIA

WILMINGTON
Ft. Fisher

Shreveport

MISSISSIPPI

Selma

Macon

GEORGIA

CHARLESTON
Ft. Sumter

VICKSBURG

JACKSON

MONTGOMERY

Red River

Grand
Gulf

Savannah

ATLANTIC OCEAN

Chattahoochee River

LOUISIANA

Port
Hudson

BATON
ROUGE

MOBILE

FLORIDA

Jacksonville

NEW ORLEANS

Pensacola

Gulf of Mexico

N

0   100   200
Miles

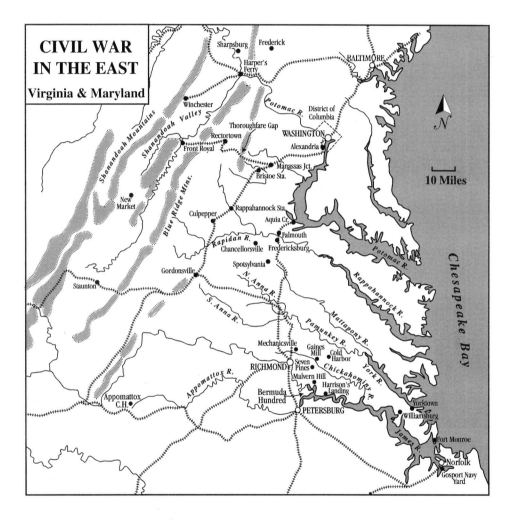

CIVIL WAR IN THE EAST

Virginia & Maryland

Sharpsburg
Frederick
BALTIMORE
Harper's Ferry
Winchester
Shanandoah Mountains
Shanandoah Valley
Potomac R.
District of Columbia
Thoroughfare Gap
WASHINGTON
Rectortown
Alexandria
Front Royal
Manassas Jct.
Bristoe Sta.
10 Miles
New Market
Blue Ridge Mtns.
Culpepper
Rappahannock Sta.
Aquia Cr.
Palmouth
Rapidan R.
Chancellorsville
Fredericksburg
Gordonsville
Spotsylvania
N. Anna R.
Rappahannock R.
Potomac R.
Chesapeake Bay
Staunton
S. Anna R.
Mattapony R.
Pamunkey R.
Mechanicsville
Gaines Mill
Cold Harbor
Seven Pines
RICHMOND
Chickahominy R.
Malvern Hill
Harrison's Landing
York R.
Appomattox R.
Bermuda Hundred
Yorktown
Appomattox C.H.
PETERSBURG
Williamsburg
James R.
Fort Monroe
Norfolk
Gosport Navy Yard

Civil War Chronology

1860

November 6   Abraham Lincoln is elected president of the United States.

December 20   South Carolina becomes the first state to secede from the Union.

1861

January-April   Mississippi, Florida, Alabama, Georgia, Louisiana, and Texas also secede from the Union.

April 1   Bombardment of Fort Sumter begins the Civil War.

April-May   Lincoln calls for volunteers to fight the Southern rebellion, causing a second wave of secession with Virginia, Arkansas, Tennessee, and North Carolina all leaving the Union.

May   Union naval forces begin blockading the Confederate coast and reoccupying some Southern ports and offshore islands.

July 21   Union forces are defeated at the battle of First Bull Run and withdraw to Washington.

1862

February   Previously unknown Union general Ulysses S. Grant captures Confederate garrisons in Tennessee at Fort Henry (February 6) and Fort Donelson (February 16).

March 7-8   Confederates and their Cherokee allies are defeated at Pea Ridge, Arkansas.

March 8-9   Naval battle at Hampton Roads, Virginia, involving the USS *Monitor* and the CSS *Virginia* (formerly the USS *Merrimac*) begins the era of the armored fighting ship.

April-July   The Union army marches on Richmond after an amphibious landing. Confederate forces block Northern advance in a series of battles. Robert E. Lee is placed in command of the main Confederate army in Virginia.

April 6-7   Grant defeats the Southern army at Shiloh Church, Tennessee, after a costly two-day battle.

April 27   New Orleans is captured by Union naval forces under Admiral David Farragut.

May 31   The battle of Seven Pines (also called Fair Oaks) is fought and the Union lines are held.

August 29-30   Lee wins substantial victory over the Army of the Potomac at the battle of Second Bull Run near Manassas, Virginia.

September 17   Union General George B. McClellan repulses Lee's first invasion of the North at Antietam Creek near Sharpsburg, Maryland, in the bloodiest single day of the war.

November 13   Grant begins operations against the key Confederate fortress at Vicksburg, Mississippi.

December 13   Union forces suffer heavy losses storming Confederate positions at Fredericksburg, Virginia.

1863

January 1   President Lincoln issues the Emancipation Proclamation, freeing the slaves in the Southern states.

May 1-6	Lee wins an impressive victory at Chancellorsville, but key Southern commander Thomas J. "Stonewall" Jackson dies of wounds, an irreplaceable loss for the Army of Northern Virginia.
June	The city of Vicksburg and the town of Port Hudson are held under siege by the Union army. They surrender on July 4.
July 1-3	Lee's second invasion of the North is decisively defeated at Gettysburg, Pennsylvania.
July 16	Union forces led by the black 54th Massachusetts Infantry attempt to regain control of Fort Sumter by attacking the Fort Wagner outpost.
September 19-20	Confederate victory at Chickamauga, Georgia, gives some hope to the South after disasters at Gettysburg and Vicksburg.

1864

February 17	A new Confederate submarine, the *Hunley,* attacks and sinks the USS *Housatonic* in the waters off Charleston.
March 9	General Grant is made supreme Union commander. He decides to campaign in the East with the Army of the Potomac while General William T. Sherman carries out a destructive march across the South from the Mississippi to the Atlantic coast.
May-June	In a series of costly battles (Wilderness, Spotsylvania, and Cold Harbor), Grant gradually encircles Lee's troops in the town of Petersburg, Richmond's railway link to the rest of the South
June 19	The siege of Petersburg begins, lasting for nearly a year until the end of the war.
August 27	General Sherman captures Atlanta and begins the "March to the Sea," a campaign of destruction across Georgia and South Carolina.
November 8	Abraham Lincoln wins reelection, ending hope of the South getting a negotiated settlement.
November 30	Confederate forces are defeated at Franklin, Tennessee, losing five generals. Nashville is soon captured (December 15-16).

1865

April 2	Major Petersburg fortifications fall to the Union, making further resistance by Richmond impossible.
April 3-8	Lee withdraws his army from Richmond and attempts to reach Confederate forces still holding out in North Carolina. Union armies under Grant and Sheridan gradually encircle him.
April 9	Lee surrenders to Grant at Appomattox, Virginia, effectively ending the war.
April 14	Abraham Lincoln is assassinated by John Wilkes Booth, a Southern sympathizer.

Union Army
Army of the Potomac
Army of the James
Army of the Cumberland

Confederate Army
Army of Northern Virginia
Army of Tennessee

Members of the 13th New York Cavalry.

The Call To Arms

On March 4, 1861, Abraham Lincoln took the oath of office as the 16th president of the United States. In his inaugural address, the new president begged the citizens of his crumbling nation, "We are not enemies, but friends. We must not be enemies." But it was too late. Southern states were already leaving the federal Union to form their own new country, the Confederate States of America. An ocean of blood would flow before the issues dividing the nation would be settled for good. Now both the North and the South had the daunting task of building a military force—war was imminent.

The states of the North, including the four slave-holding states that remained loyal to the Union—Maryland, Kentucky, Delaware, and Missouri—had a population of 20 million. The Confederate states had a population of only nine million, and nearly half of them were slaves. Because of the policy of enlisting only white males between the ages of 18 and 40, the North had 4 million men available for service and the South had only 1.1 million.

When the 11 Southern states formed the Confederacy, war fever swept the land and young men in

both the North and the South volunteered to fight against their former countrymen. At first, both sides relied upon boiling public passions to fill the military. Town meetings and patriotic rallies filled every public square and fairground throughout the land. John D. Billings of the Massachusetts state militia remembered how it was in 1861, when fevers ran high and blood had not yet been shed:

> War meetings were designed to stir lagging enthusiasm. Musicians and orators blew them- selves red in the face. . . . Sometimes, the patrio- tism of such a gathering would be wrought up so intensely by waving banners, martial and vocal music and burning eloquence that a town's quota would be filled in less than an hour. It needed only the first man to step forward. . . . [A]t last, a perfect stampede set in to sign the enlistment roll.

At the start of the war the North had only a small core army of soldiers that already belonged to the pre- war Federal military—the Old Army as it was called in both the North and South. When war came in 1861, there were just 16,000 men in the Old Army and they were scattered in 29 distant forts across the West. When Abraham Lincoln was sworn in, there were only two officers in the entire United States Army who had ever led a force as large as 1,000 men into battle. And both of those officers were more than 70 years old. So both the Union and the Confederacy had to build a fighting force almost from scratch.

On April 15, 1861, President Lincoln issued a call for 75,000 volunteers for the Union army—almost five times more men than in all of the Old Army. These vol- unteers were called up for only 90 days of service, long enough, it was thought, to defeat the Confederacy.

Three weeks later, President Lincoln asked for another 42,000 army volunteers, this time to serve for three years. Eighteen thousand men were also invited to volunteer for the United States Navy. Then by July 1861, Congress authorized recruiting one million men for three years. By the spring of 1862, there were 700,000 men wearing Yankee blue of whom 90,000 were 90-day volunteers who had reenlisted for a full three-year tour of duty.

In Harper's Weekly *of May 4, 1861, the 7th New York Regiment was depicted marching down Broadway "to embark for the war."*

A band marches in Woodstock, Virginia, calling Southern men to war.

Early in the war, the Confederacy also tried to raise only an all-volunteer army. The week that Abraham Lincoln was inaugurated president in March 1861, the Confederate Congress authorized recruitment of 100,000 volunteers for a one-year obligation. By May 1861, the South's army numbered 60,000 and another 400,000 volunteers were authorized, now for a three-year tour of duty. But the Confederacy could only provide uniforms, food, and weapons for half of them. By the end of 1861, the Confederate Congress granted a $50 bonus plus a 60-day furlough home to all one-year volunteers who agreed to reenlist.

But like in the North, the all-volunteer Confederate army was not enough. In April 1862, the South enacted the first draft law in the history of the United States, nearly one year before conscription came to the North. White men between the ages of 18 and 35 were drafted for a three-year period and the enlistment of the one-year volunteers was extended for another year. But substitutes were allowed as they would be in the North. Men made a living by selling themselves as substitutes for $300 in gold, about three years' wages in the South. The Confederate army enlisted between 50,000 and 150,000 substitutes during the war. By September 1862, manpower shortages would force the Confederacy to raise the draft age from 35 to 45. To accommodate the demands of slaveholders, the Confederate Congress granted an exemption from military service to one white man per farm—provided that farm owned at least 20 slaves. Southern soldiers whose families did not own slaves or who did not have the money to pay a substitute grumbled that these laws made the War for Southern Independence "a rich man's war and a poor man's fight."

Most of the volunteers in both the North and South were young. The average age of the Yankee soldier was 26. Three-quarters of the Union troops were under the age of 30 with 40 percent of the men in blue under 21. The largest age group in service were 18-year-olds. Though the minimum age for a combat soldier was 18, thousands enlisted who were 17 and younger. Many of them wrote the number "18" on a scrap of paper and put the paper in their shoes. That way, they could truthfully say to the army recruiters, "I am over eighteen."

A survey of the military records of 1,012,273 Union soldiers showed that at least 10,233 were younger than 18 years—773 were 15 years old, 330 were 14 years old, and 127 were only 13 years old. The most famous of the Yankee child soldiers was the drummer boy of the 22nd Michigan Infantry, John L. Clem. Since he was too young to draw military pay, the regiment chipped in and paid his soldier's wages: $13 per month.

Thousands of volunteers were too old or too sickly for the soldier's life. Of those Federal volunteers who enlisted between April 1861 and July 1862, at least one-quarter were medically unfit for military service.

Union soldier Alfred Bellard of the 5th New Jersey Volunteer Infantry would remember the recruiters' useless physical examinations of volunteers early in the war:

> [W]hen a man's name was called, he would step up to the doctor who put to him the following questions: Were you ever sick in your life? Have you got rheumatism? Have you got varicose veins, and other questions of like matters, instead of finding out for himself by actual examination whether you had or not. . . . [H]e would give us a thump on the chest, and if we weren't floored nor showed any other signs of inconvenience, we were pronounced in good condition.

Many volunteers in the North and South were not born in this country. In 1860, one-third of the country's population was foreign-born. One-fourth of the men in the Union army during the Civil War were born in other countries. The largest group of Federal soldiers born abroad were Germans, who numbered 200,000; Irish-born Union soldiers numbered 150,000; Canadian-born Federals numbered 50,000; and 45,000 British-born Federals wore the blue.

Only 9 percent of soldiers in the Confederate military were foreign-born. Louisiana contributed the largest number of foreign-born troops to the Confederacy. Texas contributed the next largest number. Because so many more "foreigners" wore Union blue than Rebel gray many Southerners believed that most of the Yankee armies were foreign mercenaries. Southern hatred was especially intense for these Federals born abroad.

The result of this mixture of age, background, nationality, and physical ability was a volunteer army

John Clem

The Drummer Boy of Shiloh

Until the eve of the 20th century, armies regularly recruited young boys for service as drummers. They were not there to merely provide music. As with bugles and fifes, drums formed an important part of the battle-field communications system, with various rolls signaling different commands. Recruiting boys for the work freed men for combat duty. As the boys got older, they could be enlisted as regular soldiers.

The romantic image of the drummer boy prompted many boys—and an occasional girl in disguise—to try to enlist, often running away from home to do so. Officially, drummer boys, were supposed to be at least 12, but boys as young as 10 were sometimes found beating the "long roll" to call the men to action.

The most famous drummer of the Civil War was John Clem, who ran away from home at the age of 10, adopted "Lincoln" as a middle name, and tried to enlist as a soldier. Although he was turned down in his attempt to enlist in the 3rd Ohio, Clem followed the regiment anyway and was eventually taken on as an unofficial drummer by several regiments in succession.

Although it is unclear what regiment he was with when the Confederates attacked at Shiloh on April 6, 1862, he certainly made his presence known, beating out signals until his drum was blown to bits and then joining the soldiers. He was nicknamed "The Drummer Boy of Shiloh" and "Johnny Shiloh."

After Shiloh, Clem tagged along with the 24th Ohio, the 22nd Wisconsin, and finally the 22nd Michigan, in which he was formally enlisted as a drummer boy in May 1863, having attained the requisite age of 12. That September, Clem served at Chickamauga, toting a special short musket, with which he

John Clem

pursued, wounded, and captured a Confederate colonel.

A few weeks later, Clem was captured and spent two months as an honored prisoner of the Confederate army. After his release he was, for a time, a courier to Major General George Thomas, for whom he had drummed at Chickamauga, and later served in the Atlanta campaign, during which he was twice wounded. Clem was discharged in September 1864.

After the war, Clem attempted to win an appointment to West Point, but having been otherwise occupied when most boys his age were in school, he was unable to pass the entrance examination. With the support of President Ulysses S. Grant, for whom he had drummed at Shiloh, he was given a direct commission as a second lieutenant in the 24th Infantry in 1871. Clem served on the frontier for many years, transferring to the Quartermaster Corps in the 1890s. In 1916, he retired as a major general, the last Civil War veteran on active duty. Clem died in 1937.

Volunteers were sworn in throughout the North: "I,____, do solemnly swear that I will bear true allegiance to the United States of America; that I will serve them honestly and faithfully against all enemies or opposers whatsoever . . . "

of unfit men who knew nothing of military service. In December 1861, Union General Henry Halleck reported to General-in-Chief Winfield Scott in Washington, "This, General, is no army, but rather a military rabble." The crisis of turning this group into a military force began immediately. Before these men in blue and gray could fight and die on bloodsoaked hillsides with names like Shiloh, Antietam, Chickamauga, Fredericksburg, and Gettysburg, they had to become a real army.

II

Learning the Drill

*T*ens of thousands of young men, who knew nothing about soldiering beyond the cheerful brass bands that welcomed them at the recruiting stations, poured into the armies. In October 1861, then-Colonel John Beatty of the Union's 3rd Ohio Volunteer Infantry described the new men flooding into training camp: "The men are good, stout, hearty, intelligent fellows and will make excellent soldiers. But they have now no regard for their officers and, as a rule, do as they please." One month earlier, Private John Holloway of the 1st Georgia Volunteer Infantry wrote home with his first impression of training the Confederate army: "I believe men can stand most anything after they get used to it. The hardest part is getting used to it."

Learning the language of soldiering and the maneuvers required of infantry began with drills by small groups of foot soldiers. Drilling consisted of marching while learning to execute military commands and weapon maneuvers—repeating them over and over until perfected. Gradually, daily drill would include formations by company, by regiment, and by brigade. Drilling under the weight of a knapsack and a 12-pound rifle was the new recruit's first taste of soldier

life. To Yankee Oliver W. Norton, life was one long drill: "The first thing in the morning is drill, then drill, then drill again. Then drill, drill, and a little more drill. Then drill and lastly, drill. Between drills, we drill and sometimes stop to eat a little and have roll-call." In the 2nd Rhode Island Volunteer Infantry, 19-year-old Corporal Elisha Hunt Rhodes wrote in his diary in April 1861, "We drill day and night."

Alfred Bellard of the 5th New Jersey Volunteer Infantry remembered five hours of drill every day during his early service with the Federals in 1861. Many recruits in both armies could not tell their left foot from their right foot which made it difficult to learn to march and drill. So their veteran instructors put a flake of hay on one of their feet and a sprig of straw on the other. Men marched to the cadence call of "Straw foot! Hay foot!"

A company of Yankee soldiers stands at attention as part of their daily drill routine.

The vast majority of every soldier's time during the Civil War was not spent in combat. Time was measured by the beat of the drum or the bugle call which

marked each day's tiresome routine. Colonel Beatty called it the "monotony of the camp." Tired, homesick soldiers awoke to the drum beat or bugle call of reveille at 5:00 in the morning (6:00 during the dead of winter), then breakfast call at 6:00 (an hour later in winter), followed an hour later by the surgeon's call for sick men to report to camp physicians. For the three hours between 8:00 and 11:00, soldiers drilled. Recall sounded at 11:00 with lunch at noon—if there was food to eat. Then another afternoon of drill, ending with the 5:00 bugle call of recall. Another drum or bugle call signaled the assignment of guard duties at

Reveille was usually drummed at 5:00 in the morning, when weary soldiers had to rise to another day of drilling, marching, or battle.

21

5:30. "Tattoo" was blown at 9:00 with each regiment's sergeants completing the roll-call of men present for duty. The day finally ended at 9:30 when the mournful notes of "Taps" were blown over exhausted men in blue or gray. A routine day without meeting the enemy would have at least 12 different bugle calls or drum beats.

It did not take long for the new men to forget the hometown military parades and speeches which had driven them into the recruiters' open arms. "After a time," remembered William M. Haigh of the 36th Illinois Volunteer Infantry,

> the incessant drill and standing guard beneath a broiling sun or in a drenching rain storm, washing greasy dishes, scouring rusty knives, cooking and eating stale beef, and at night wallowing down to sleep ten in a tent, pretty effectually took the romance out of camp life and left it a very plain, drudging and stupid reality.

Confederate Carlton McCarthy of the Richmond Howitzers, quickly learned that crossing sabers with Yankees was not what training camp was about:

> Another fancy idea was that the principal occupation of a soldier should be actual conflict with the enemy. They didn't dream of such a thing as camping for six months at a time without firing a gun, or marching and countermarching to mislead the enemy, or driving wagons and ambulances, building bridges, currying horses, and the thousand commonplace duties of the soldier.

Soldier life meant tedium and hard work, not fighting the enemy. During its first two years, the Yankee

Army of the Potomac fought Rebels for a total of only 30 days.

As new men trained and adjusted to army life, the armies of both the North and the South followed the Old Army model for infantry organization: 100 men formed a company; 10 companies formed a regiment; 4 regiments formed a brigade; 3 or 4 brigades formed a division; 2 or 3 divisions formed a corps. But the thousand-man regiments quickly dwindled as disease and battle thinned the ranks. After Gettysburg in July 1863, the average Union regiment counted only 375 men.

Along with learning drills and bugle calls, the new armies learned their weapons. For the new nation of the Confederacy, finding sufficient weapons for the army was a continuous crisis. When war began in April 1861, the South had on hand 130,000 Revolutionary War-era, smoothbore muskets and only

Soldiers from the 1st Maine Cavalry practice firing their rifles.

20,000 of the new, rifled muskets. Smoothbore muskets fired a lead ball, slightly larger than a half inch in diameter. But smooth musket barrels were accurate for a range of only 80 yards. Cutting grooves on the inside of the barrels to make a "rifled" musket greatly increased accuracy by spinning the musket's bullet, either round ball or conical. A rifled musket was accurate and deadly out to 400 yards. The Northern and Southern infantries used the Springfield and Enfield rifled muskets as the infantryman's weapon of choice. Although the Union blockade of Southern seaports cut off much Confederate commerce with England, the Confederacy was able to purchase 100,000 Enfields during the war. Once armies clashed in bloody combat, the Confederacy was able to increase its supply of rifles by picking up Yankee rifles from the battlefields. Soldiers on both sides were impressed with their modern rifles. "Our Enfield rifles," wrote Lieutenant Colonel Samuel Beardsley of the 24th New York Volunteer Infantry, "are a terrible weapon, being able to kill a man at the distance of a mile."

Next to drilling, marching, and learning new weapons, the hardest lesson soldiers learned in camp was the devastating effect of disease. In the South, malaria could cripple a corps. As Yankee divisions invaded the Confederacy, Southern mosquitos reaped their toll through uniforms of blue and gray. Malaria caused 20 percent of all serious illness during the war. Especially among Yankee farmboys, measles was also a deadly killer. Recruits from congested, eastern cities had a natural immunity to the disease from having it as children. But men from the farms had never lived in such close quarters and army camps in the North and the South became vast measles hospitals. During the summer of 1861, more than 200 Southern soldiers died from measles in Mississippi camps.

Drilling, marching, disease, and tedium worked to forge untrained strangers into effective armies. Some new men thrived and some did not. "Camp life is dull," Elisha Hunt Rhodes wrote in August 1861 of his Rhode Islanders, "but I suppose that is part of a soldier's duty."

Once sufficiently drilled to march in search of the enemy, armies North and South put 100,000 men on the road. Such an infantry force had to drag along with it 2,500 supply wagons, at least 35,000 horses and mules, and 600 tons of supplies per day. On thousands of miles of dirt roads, infantry marched generally at "route step" of about two-and-a-half miles per hour, stopping for a 10-minute rest every hour. Troops quickly found that their government-issue knapsacks, haversacks, overcoats, and blanket rolls were too much to carry with their heavy rifles. Both sides soon learned to travel light. Private Robert Hale Strong of

A battery of Federal soldiers fords a stream on the day of the battle of Second Bull Run in August 1862.

the 105th Illinois Volunteers felt on the march that "the straps of my knapsack would pull my shoulders out of joint. The straps of my haversack and canteen seemed no bigger than a thread and were cutting the tops of my shoulders. My gun seemed to weigh a ton." Men soon threw away all unnecessary equipment on long marches. Confederate Carlton McCarthy remembered:

> Reduced to the minimum, the private soldier consisted of one man, one hat, one jacket, one shirt, one pair of pants, one pair of drawers, one pair of shoes, and one pair of socks. His baggage was one blanket, one rubber blanket, and one haversack. The haversack generally contained smoking tobacco and a pipe and a small piece of soap.

By the spring of 1864, the blue Army of the Potomac numbered 120,000 men, 274 horse-drawn cannons, 835 horse-drawn ambulances, 4,300 supply wagons, and at least 56,000 horses and mules. Had the supply wagons traveled single-file in search of Robert E. Lee, that wagon train would have been 75 miles long.

Trained, drilled, and on the march, the new armies headed into the field to fight and die for their countries. Leaving training camp, the men thought they knew what soldier life was about. But they did not know and could not know until they experienced camp life on the march, smelled their first battlefield, and confronted the foot soldier's real worst enemy—rain.

III

Becoming Veterans

*O*nce enlisted as a volunteer or drafted as a conscript, the new soldier quickly learned that rain was his first enemy. "Rain was the greatest discomfort a soldier could have," wrote Carlton McCarthy, a soldier in Robert E. Lee's army. "It was more uncomfortable than the severest cold with clear weather: wet clothes, shoes and blankets; wet meat and bread; wet feet and wet ground; wet wood to burn, or rather not to burn."

To keep the rain off when not on the march, the foot soldier's home was his tent. Several kinds of canvas tents were used in both armies. The "wall tent" was the largest. It had vertical, rectangular walls with a tall sloping roof. Spacious but cumbersome to take down and move quickly, the wall tents were quickly restricted to field hospitals which did not have to move as fast as the armies.

The next smaller tent was the popular Sibley tent, named for Confederate Brigadier General Henry Sibley who had invented them in the Old Army. The Sibley was a "teepee" standing 12 feet high. Its rounded base was 18 feet across. A stove pipe poked

through the center point. Rather unwieldy like the wall tent, the Sibley was not much used in the field after the first year of the war.

Very common on both sides was the "wedge tent." It is the familiar camping tent with sloping sides fastened into the ground and supported by a centerline, horizontal beam. The wedge tent was six feet long and slept four soldiers in seven square feet of space. It was not large enough for a fire and had no chimney like the Sibley tent.

But the most common tent, the tent remembered by all foot soldiers in blue and gray, was the humble "shelter tent"—known then and through all of America's wars since as the dog tent or "pup tent." During the Civil War, nearly all infantrymen slept in pup tents in the spring, summer, and fall. Each infantryman carried half of a full shelter tent. When

This photo of an encampment of the Army of the James in Virginia shows the tents used by some of the soldiers, with earthworks behind them for protection.

Men of the 5th Georgia Regiment stand before their well-supplied tent at the beginning of the long war.

two soldiers fastened their halves together with buttons or hooks, it formed a small, sloping tent six feet long and only four feet wide. Open at both ends, the shelter tent slept two men. If a third could squeeze inside, his "half" of the tent would be used to seal off one of the open ends.

Because soldiers did not appreciate their tiny tents, open to the wind and rain at each end, they quickly named the shelter tent a "puppy tent." Both sides of the war found thousands of cold, wet soldiers writing on the sides of their pup tent to show their displeasure. Tents by the hundreds bore crude letters spelling "Puppies for Sale" or "Rat Terriers." And in the dreadful rain, Elisha Hunt Rhodes remembered, a pup tent "makes a regular shower bath."

The Confederacy made regular use of the Sibleys, wedge tents, and pup tents. But it was more common for Rebels to sleep without tents except in the severest

This photo shows a soldier's tent set up using materials from the woods surrounding the camp, outside Petersburg, Virginia, in August of 1864.

winter. "Tents were rarely seen," Carlton McCarthy recalled of the Army of Northern Virginia. "Two men slept together, each having a blanket and an oil-cloth. One oil-cloth went next to the ground. The two laid on this, covered themselves with two blankets, protected from the rain with the second oil-cloth on top, and slept very comfortably through rain, snow and hail."

When not pursuing Yankees or being chased by Yankees, Confederates also built two-sided tents from items scrounged from the countryside. They called them "shebangs." The shebang had two sides supported by a single, horizontal beam supported by end posts stuck in the ground. The sloping sides were covered with canvas, barn siding, or tree bark and brush.

Harsh winters in the East forced both sides to abandon winter operations. The Union and Confederate armies generally went into "winter camp" when heavy snows came. For months at a time, opposing armies would go into winter quarters, often close enough for troops to hear the activities in the enemy's camp. Months in one place allowed the weary foot soldiers to build comfortable winter shelters, sometimes of rough hewn logs with chimneys and indoor fires. Often, the reliable old pup tent was pressed into winter service when the canvas tent was draped over the outside logs. Soldiers poured water on the canvas so it would freeze for better insulation.

Since much of the reality of war was waiting and marching instead of fighting, camp life accounted for the vast majority of a soldier's army career. With young men camping together by tens of thousands, there was no shortage of good cheer even in the face of disease, harsh weather, and miserable food. Colonel John Beatty

The army tried to make winter quarters more solid for as many soldiers as possible. These were some of the quarters of the Army of the Potomac in February 1864.

remembered the good times of Yankee camp life which could become rowdy and noisy: "Camp life to a young man who has nothing especially to tie him to home has many attractions—abundance of company, continual excitement, and all the fun and frolic that a thousand light-hearted boys can devise."

Music was everywhere. The longer that regiments and divisions were camped on the same campground, the more regular the music became. Regimental bands were common and most welcome for breaking the tedium. Even General Robert E. Lee knew the value of army bands for military morale. He once said, "I don't believe we can have an army without music." Camping in Tennessee in February 1862, Colonel Beatty acknowledged that "the martial band of the regiment is doing its utmost to keep the boys in good spirits."

Men and teenagers far from home welcomed the sad, sweet tunes which were the most popular in the camps of the North and South. Soldiers stopped

The band of the 30th Pennsylvania Reserves.

scrubbing pots and pans or cleaning their weapons when some regimental band struck up "When This Cruel War Is Over" or the sad song of farewell, "Lorena." But by far, the favorite song at any time in any army was "Home, Sweet Home."

Often, the enemy armies were so close to each other in camp that each side could hear the other side's band. Many times, before and after battles of unspeakable bloodshed, each side's band would deliberately serenade the other side. "Dueling bands" would compete for the best rendition of "Home, Sweet Home." It happened after the battle of Murfreesburo in Tennessee in 1863. And it happened at Christmastime 1862 at Fredericksburg, Virginia, after General Lee's Confederate army had slaughtered the courageous Federals who had attacked uphill.

Young soldiers who had seen thousands of their friends and fellow soldiers killed or crippled before

HOME, SWEET HOME

'Mid pleasures and palaces though we may roam,
Be it ever so humble, there's no place like home;
A charm from the skies seems to hallow us there,
Which seek thro' the world, is ne'er met with elsewhere.
Home! Home! sweet, sweet Home!
There's no place like Home!
There's no place like Home!

An exile from home, splendor dazzles in vain,
Oh! give me my lowly thatched cottage again;
The birds singing gaily that came at my call;
Give me them, with the peace of mind, dearer than all.
(Chorus)

To thee, I'll return, overburdened with care,
The heart's dearest solace will smile on me there.
No more from that cottage again will I roam,
Be it ever so humble, there's no place like home. (Chorus)

their eyes were sometimes struck in the heart by their own band's music. When the Federal army went into winter camp in late 1863 in Virginia, so many men cried when they heard "Home, Sweet Home," that the Union generals banned the song from camp.

To lighten the tedium of life in camp, many men turned to gambling of all kinds. To break the monotony, gambling and wagering were rampant. By 1864, there was so much gambling in the Yankees' Army of the James that the force became known as the "Army of the Games." Contraband alcohol was drunk by many lonesome soldiers. If men could not buy liquor, they made their own. It was known affectionately on both sides as "Tanglefoot" or "Oh Be Joyful."

And wherever young men make camp at any time in any war, there is good humor to help cope with mili-

Officers of the 114th Infantry play cards outside Petersburg, Virginia, in August of 1864. Gambling was one of the favorite pastimes of the Civil War soldiers in camp.

tary hardship. Carlton McCarthy remembered that every Rebel camp had its usual cast of characters who helped others to cope and to survive with good cheer. Private McCarthy remembered well that each regiment had its valuable man known as the Scribe:

The Scribe was a wonderful fellow and very useful. He could write a two-hours' pass, sign the captain's name better than the captain himself, and endorse it "respectfully forwarded, approved," sign the colonel's name after "respectfully forwarded, approved," and then on up to the commanding officer.

And there was the common soldier's graveyard humor, used by all to hide the fear and the homesickness. In June 1864 when General Grant's Federal army laid siege to Petersburg, Virginia, on the outskirts of Richmond, 22-year-old Lieutenant Elisha Hunt Rhodes wrote in his diary about one Yankee's way of amusing himself:

> Yesterday, Sergeant Major George F. Polley, 10th Massachusetts Volunteers, showed me a board on which he had carved his name, date of birth, and had left a place for the date of his death. . . . I asked him if he expected to be killed and he said No, and that he had made his head board only for fun. Today, he was killed by a shell fired from a Rebel battery.

On every soldier's mind in every army was the daily monotony of army food. The most prized possession was coffee. The Yankees had it, but the Federal blockade of Southern seaports generally stopped the flow of coffee to the South. Likewise, the war stopped the sale of Southern tobacco to the North. A common sight when enemy armies camped in sight of each other were flags of truce among the private soldiers who would slip between the lines to trade Yankee coffee for Rebel tobacco.

Army coffee was issued "green." Green coffee beans had to be roasted over open fires. Then rifle butts or bayonet handles were used to pound the toasted beans into coffee to be boiled. Federal foot soldiers carried their cracked, roasted coffee in a little bag with sugar already added so the whole precious mixture could be thrown into an available pot of boiling water.

The mainstay of a soldier's diet in the Civil War was hardtack: a rock-hard soda cracker, three inches square and half an inch thick. More often than not, the hardtack was full of worms. Soldiers called their crackers, "worm castles" or "tooth dullers." Hardtack came in boxes stamped "BC" for Brigade Commissary. But the soldiers knew better: they said the initials stood for the date when the crackers were manufactured. Hardtack was too hard to eat raw, unless they could be broken with rifle butts. So they were used to thicken many camp recipes. Yankees used hardtack to make "skillygalee"—a dish in which hardtack was soaked in water until soft and then browned with pork fat in frying pans. Boys in blue also made hish

Soldiers of the 93rd New York Infantry eating in camp in August 1863.

stew—a thick soup of hardtack, pork or beef, dried vegetables, garlic, and salt. When pepper could be found, hish became "hell-fire stew."

The reality of camp life was poor rations or decent rations poorly prepared. Alfred Bellard remembered the fare of the 5th New Jersey Volunteers:

> Our soup, coffee and meat were boiled in camp kettles suspended over the fire which were also used for boiling our dirty clothes. Not a very nice thing for a soup pot, especially when they were full of vermin as they were most of the time when on active service. Our stomachs were strong enough, however, to stand it.

In the Southern armies, especially during the last two years of the war, even hardtack would have been a luxury. War and the blockade cut off hardtack supplies. So cornmeal and cornbread became the heart of Confederate camp cooking. While their enemies in blue made hish, the Confederates made cush, a concoction of crumbled cornbread, water, and raw beef or pork, all stewed in a vat of bacon grease.

By the third and fourth year of the Civil War, food shortages turned into hunger, which became starvation in many Confederate camps. During General Grant's 47-day siege of Vicksburg, Mississippi, which fell to Union forces in July 1863, hunger tormented the Confederate defenders as much as Yankee artillery. Soldiers ate dogs and rats when military food was exhausted. The daily meat ration for the Rebels was one-third of the ration fed soldiers near Richmond, and half of that ration was mule meat. Confederate bread rations were really ground peas, and camp cooks made soup from boiled grass.

Confederate soldiers were often reduced to taking the rations from the bodies of dead Federals. Carlton McCarthy remembered:

> The most melancholy eating a soldier was ever forced to do was, when pinched with hunger, cold, wet and dejected, he wandered over the deserted field of battle and satisfied his cravings with the contents of the haversacks of the dead. If there is anything which will overcome the natural abhorrence which a man feels for the enemy, the loathing of the bloated dead, and the awe engendered by the presence of death, solitude and silence, it is hunger.

And when shoes and clothing also gave out among hungry Confederates, many resorted to taking them from the bodies of dead Yankees, as Lieutenant John Burnham of the 16th Connecticut Volunteers saw in September 1862, on the battlefield of Antietam in Maryland:

> The pockets of all our dead were emptied. In some instances, they cut the pockets out of the clothing, not stopping to examine them on the field. The shoes, too, were taken from all our dead bodies. . . . I saw as many as five hundred prisoners. . . . [T]heir faces were thin and cadaverous as though they had been starved to death.

Confederates often joked in their camps that "all a Yankee is worth is his shoes." The shortage of shoes grew worse as the war ground on. By the end of 1862, as many as 40,000 Confederates were barefoot just in Robert E. Lee's Army of Northern Virginia. When

General John Bell Hood marched his weary Rebels through Tennessee in the winter of 1864-1865, his men left bloody footprints in the snow between Franklin and Nashville.

Bad shoes or no shoes was also a painful reality to the Federals who had to march on foot to invade and conquer the Confederate States of America. The Confederacy included 750,000 square miles—twice the size of the 13 original colonies. During the February 1862 march to Nashville, John Beatty felt for his Ohioans' sore feet: "The feet of the men [are] badly blistered and the regiment limps along in wretched style. . . . Many of the boys have no shoes." When Yankees did have boots, Virginia rain in 1862 made the boots miserable. Alfred Bellard remembered:

Members of the 22nd New York State Militia of Company D stand in front of their tent that they named "The Rendezvous."

> I had on a pair of tight boots. By the time we encamped, they had become so tight from being wet, that I could not pull them off. As sand had got into them some way, I was hardly able to walk. As there was no way of pulling them off, some of the men cut them off with knives. When they did come off at last, some of the skin went with them. There being no clothing with the army, I had to get a pair of dead men's shoes from the battlefield.

The Confederates were not alone in food shortages. Hunger was also known by the Union soldiers. The worst occurred in June and July 1863 during the fighting around Chattanooga, Tennessee. The Federal supply lines were thin and vulnerable to Confederate attack. Men in blue called the unreliable supply trail the "cracker line" since it brought them their hardtack. So many Federals were hungry that guards were posted to keep foot soldiers from stealing the grain reserved for the horses and mules. Brigadier General John Beatty wrote of the Chattanooga campaign in November 1863: "There has been much suffering among the men. They have for weeks been reduced to quarter rations, and at time so eager for food that . . . they have picked up the grains of corn from the mud where mules have been fed." Union infantryman Robert Hale Strong of the 105th Illinois Volunteers knew the same hunger during General Sherman's 1864 "March to the Sea" across Georgia. "I have stolen the corn from the mules and horses after it had been put in their boxes, washed their slobber off of it, and parched and eaten it."

In the field, fresh and clean water was often harder to find than healthful food. With 75,000 to 125,000 men on the march, sanitation was nearly impossible. The medical science of the day knew nothing of bacteria. Robert Hale Strong recorded a very personal experience with contaminated drinking water during a nighttime walk to the creek:

> It was my turn to procure water to cook our supper. . . . I was fortunate to find an old log extending a little ways into the creek, so I stood on the log and filled our vessels. We made coffee, ate our supper, and went to bed. The next morning, I went back by daylight for water . . . and found

that the "log" that I stood on the night before was a dead and rotting mule. It was raining and the rain had been running off the mule's body and our coffee had been partly mule soup.

Beyond foul weather, bad food or no food, and foul drinking water, the camp of soldiers in the field was unhealthy from filth, disease, and insects. Neither side was immune from dirt. "In the southern camp," wrote Confederate H. V. Redfield, "you could hardly go twenty steps without getting into filth of some sort. . . . Much of the sickness which scourged the Southern army, particularly in the early stages of the war, is attributable no doubt to the filthy conditions of their camps." Federals had it no better. Samuel Fiske of the 14th Connecticut Volunteers would remember that "The first observation every man would make is that the soldier's life is an eminently dirty one. . . . [D]irt steadily and surely prevails till a regiment appears like a regiment of ragamuffins."

From filth and hunger came disease. The worst was typhoid fever which killed 17,000 Confederate soldiers during one 18-month period. Smallpox erupted in the South during the war's middle years. Just in hospitals in Richmond, Virginia, during a two-and-a-half-year period, at least 1,020 Rebel soldiers died from smallpox.

Northerners also suffered from camp disease. When his Ohio regiment was camped in Kentucky, John Beatty wrote in his wartime diary during the winter of 1862: "Passing through the company quarters of our regiment at midnight, I was alarmed by the constant and heavy coughing of the men. I fear the winter will send many more men to the grave than the bullets of the enemy." And while in winter quarters during the winter of 1862-63 at Fredericksburg, Virginia, S.

Men of Company B in September of 1864, during the siege of Petersburg.

Millett Thompson of the 13th New Hampshire Volunteers wrote that, "This camp of 100,000 men is practically a vast hospital."

Because of camp disease and Confederate bullets, the Federal army created an entire corps of sick or wounded men. These walking wounded were grouped together into a unit first called the Invalid Corps in April 1863. By the end of 1863, more than 20,000 men limped along in the Invalid Corps. In March 1864, someone in Washington realized that the corps' initials, "IC," were also used to stamp wornout equipment ready for the junk pile—the initials stood for "Inspected: condemned." When Washington thought that using the same initials for the Invalid Corps might be bad for morale, the corps was renamed the Veteran Reserve Corps. Its convalescents were used behind the lines for administrative, hospital, or guard duties.

Certainly the most annoying aspect of camp life in both the North and South, was the constant presence of lice. The famous chaplain of the Union's Irish Brigade, Father William Corby, called camp lice a "pestilence worse in nature than many of the Egyptian plagues."

The tiny lice which tormented the armies were called "graybacks" by the men. It was common for a soldier to pick 50 lice from his body at one sitting. Robert Hale Strong did not lose his good humor when remembering his Yankee lice: "They would get into the seams of our shirts and pants and drawers, and when not engaged in laying eggs, would sally out and forage off our defenseless bodies. Next, he, his children and his children's children, with their brothers and sisters, would hold squad drill on our backs." Some Confederates found the lice so offensive that they could only conclude that they were a deliberate infestation planned by the Yankees. "The grayback was never here until Lincoln's soldiers came," argued Lieutenant Albert T. Goodloe of the 35th Alabama Infantry, "and the easy presumption is that they brought him along with them and turned him loose on us."

Endless marches, lice, disease, hunger, putrid water, and enemy shot and shell flying over head gradually turned new soldiers into grizzled veterans—especially after, one by one, they had "seen the elephant"—combat.

Soldiers of the North . . .

. . . and soldiers of the South pose before going into battle.

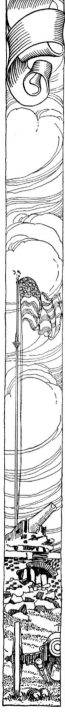

IV

"Seeing the Elephant"

*F*rom the brass bands and the recruiters' smiling faces, young men and teenage boys marched off to training camps in the North and South. They learned military drills, military courtesy, and how to live with bad food, contaminated water, disease, and homesickness. And, one by one, they waited to learn how they would react the first time the air was thick with the smoke of gunpowder. Old hands called their first combat experience "seeing the elephant." Tens of thousands of young men would see the elephant only once—and die.

For many, life in camp began as one grand and glorious adventure. Writing in his diary on the very day of his 20th birthday, young Sergeant Elisha Hunt Rhodes must have smiled in March 1862 when he penned, "Sleeping on the ground is fun, and a bed of pine boughs better than one of feathers."

But once each soldier saw the elephant and heard the cries of the wounded and maimed, something happened to him. "I cannot describe the change nor do I know when it took place," wrote Private Henry Graves, a Confederate soldier, in June 1862. "I know

that there is a change, for I look on the carcass of a man now with pretty much such feeling as I would do were it a horse or hog."

With the hardness of battle comes a dreadful clarity of vision, also seen by all young men in all wars. Weary, hungry, footsore soldiers slowly realize that they are food for that elephant. Yankee Sergeant Robert T. Goodyear of the 27th Connecticut Volunteers realized it by February 1863 when he wrote home:

> The soldier of today has a keen perception. He has been educated for a different calling and he is not slow to detect the real character of the war as it is conducted. Abused, humbugged, imposed upon and frequently half-starved and sick, he sees himself made a mere tool for political speculators to operate with. Led on to slaughter and defeat by drunken and incompetent officers, he has become disheartened, discouraged, demoralized.

The loneliness of camp life did not help that discouragement. "You have no idea how lonesome I feel this day," Dr. James M. Holloway of the 18th Mississippi Volunteers wrote home on Christmas Day, 1861. He began his letter, "My Dear Wife and Babies."

The one great comfort to all soldiers in Civil War camps was the writing of letters home, and the receiving of letters from their families. Letters to and from Union soldiers camped in the East were processed in Washington. Some 45,000 pieces of mail from soldiers went to Washington every day. Yankees fighting in the West sent their mail through Louisville, Kentucky, where 70,000 letters were forwarded every day. Some regiments generated 600 letters each day.

Soldiers pause to read letters from home and remember those who wrote them.

Once soldiers had seen the elephant and once they became hardened to the sights of the battlefield, their letters reflected the pain and suffering all around them. Where the men camped and wrote was reflected in the mail home. The Irish Brigade's famous priest, Father Corby, remembered camping at Savage's Station, Virginia, during the battle of the Seven Days in June and July 1862. "Many dead bodies were removed to make room to build camp fires for cooking purposes, and in many cases, the dying and the dead were placed in the same pile."

From camps such as this, Confederate Captain William Nugent of the 28th Mississippi Cavalry wrote home in September 1863 in a letter addressed to "My Darling Wife":

> The idea of being continually employed in the destruction of human life is revolting in the extreme. Necessity, imperious and exacting, forces us along and we hurry through the dreadful task,

apparently unconscious of its demoralizing influences and destructive effects both upon the nation and individuals.

Private James M. Binford in the 21st Virginia Volunteers wrote of seeing the elephant in August 1862: "I have had enough of the glory of war. I am sick of seeing dead men and men's limbs torn from their bodies."

For the veterans in the field, camp life after battle required the burial of the dead, sometimes by the thousands. Alfred Bellard of the 5th New Jersey Volunteers did burial duty after the battle of Fair Oaks (also known as Seven Pines) in early June 1862:

The dead Rebs were still lying where they fell on the second day after the battle and presented a horrible sight. They had swelled to double their natural size, and as a consequence, their clothing had burst. . . . Upon finding a body, a hole was

Soldiers lay dead in the woods near Little Round Top, Gettysburg, Pennsylvania, in July 1863.

dug about 18 inches deep close to him, two or three pieces of wood or fence rails were placed under the body, and at the word "Roll" rolled in, the men taking to their heels the instant it went over the edge, for in nearly all cases it burst upon striking bottom.

Robert Hale Strong of the 105th Illinois Volunteers also drew burial detail. "Some had been dead for three or four days, and the flesh would not hold together to lift them. So we put them in blankets, or tied the legs of their pants and their coatsleeves together and gently dragged them to their last resting place."

Veterans in camp knew that the grim work of the burial details could be ruined by the ever present rain. The battle of the Wilderness in May 1864, in Virginia, was a two-day slaughter. When the 105th Illinois Volunteers marched across that battlefield one year after the battle, Robert Hale Strong saw that the dead had not stayed buried: "At the Battle of the Wilderness scene, we marched for hours over the battlefield. . . . The dead had been buried where they fell . . . Here and there an arm or leg or a hand or foot would stick out. . . . [T]he boys would kick a skull out of the way as indifferently as if it had been a stone."

Union volunteer Alfred Bellard saw what rain could do to the Fair Oaks (Seven Pines) burial ground: "The rain also washed the dirt from the shallow graves and every morning a detail was sent out to cover up arms, legs, and heads that had protruded from the ground during the night." Such sights moved soldiers to consider the larger questions of life. As the war dragged on through four bloody years, religion played an important role in camp.

Especially on the march to battle, whole armies would throw away the evidence of "sin" when sudden death might be only hours away. Yankee Jesse B. Young looked to the side of the dirt road which led to the December 1862 slaughter of Union soldiers at the battle of Fredericksburg: "On the way over, I noticed here and there packs of cards and empty whisky bottles strewn by the roadside. Soldiers did not relish the idea of being shot with packs of the one or flasks of the other on their persons."

The United States Christian Commission worked throughout the war to minister to the religious and spiritual needs of the Federal armies. Formed at the beginning of the war, the Christian Commission had distributed 570,000 Bibles and nearly 5 million hymn books to Union troops in its first three years. The American Bible Society in the North even sent 100,000 Bibles down to Confederate regiments. The British Bible Society also supplied Bibles and hymnals to the South. Often, soldiers had to minister to their religious needs by themselves. Official army chaplains were scarce. By the middle of the war, one-third of Union infantry regiments had no chaplains at all. In the Confederate armies, half of the regiments did not have a chaplain. A brigadier general of his Ohio regiment by 1863, John Beatty saw Union troops build their own camp chapel with tree limbs in Tennessee:

> The new moon favors us with just sufficient light to reveal fully the great oaks, the white tents, and the shadowy outline of the Cumberland Mountains. The pious few of the 88th Indiana, assembled in a booth constructed of branches, are breathing out the devotional inspirations and aspirations in an old hymn which carries us back to the churches and homes of the civilized world.

In January 1864, Lieutenant Elisha Hunt Rhodes described the 2nd Rhode Island Volunteer Infantry's new, homemade chapel at camp near Brandy Station, Virginia:

> Tonight we dedicated our new chapel . . . [W]e have named it Hope Chapel. The building is made of logs hewn smooth on one side . . . . The roof is covered by a large canvas. . . . A chandelier made from old tin cans, or the tin taken from cans, is in the center . . . [T]he ground or floor is carpeted with pine boughs.

Religion certainly played a vital role in camp life among Confederates. One month into the war, Confederate President Jefferson Davis was authorized by the Confederate Congress to appoint field chaplains, one per regiment. Their pay was $85 per month but they had to buy their own horses and their own food in camp and on the march.

Homemade chapels grew especially fast during the long, gray months of winter quarters when entire armies made camp to wait out the cold. At winter quarters during the winter of 1863-1864, Robert E. Lee's Army of Northern Virginia built at least 60 chapels in their Virginia camps. Some 15,000 soldiers were baptized beside the frozen Rapidan River. General Lee was so impressed with his army's religious fervor that on Sunday, February 7, 1864, he issued an order acknowledging that "he has learned with great pleasure that in many brigades convenient houses of worship have been erected, and [he] earnestly desires that every facility consistent with the requirements of discipline shall be afforded the men to assemble themselves together for the purpose of devotion."

Chaplains of the Ninth Corps pose in October 1864.

Chaplains were also on the battlefields when the bullets flew. Perhaps the most illustrious was Father William Corby who wore the blue. During the heat of combat at the three-day battle of Gettysburg in July 1863, Father Corby gave absolution and blessing under fire to the Irish Brigade of the Union's Third Corps. Major General St. Clair Mulholland witnessed Father Corby's heroic act on July 2, the second day of the battle:

> Father Corby stood on a large rock in front of the brigade. Addressing the men, he explained what he was about to do, saying that each one could receive the benefit of absolution by making a sincere Act of Contrition and firmly resolving to embrace the first opportunity of confessing his sins. . . . As he closed his address, every man, Catholic and non-Catholic, fell on his knees with his head bowed down. Then, stretching his right hand toward the brigade, Father Corby pronounced the words of absolution. . . . The scene was more than impressive: it was awe-inspiring . . . . In less than half an hour, many of them were numbered with the dead of July 2.

After his service with the Army of the Potomac, Father Corby became president of the University of

Notre Dame. A bronze statue of Father Corby blessing his Irishmen still stands at the university.

But religion in camp did not mean that army discipline would cease to be a constant problem. Although the veterans of camp would learn how to be soldiers, their status as civilian volunteers or reluctant draftees continued to demand a firm hand by their officers. In January 1862, John Beatty sized up his ill-disciplined Ohioans: "Very many of these soldiers think they should be allowed to work when they please, play when they please, and, in short, do as they please. Until this idea is expelled from their minds, the regiment will be but little if any better than a mob."

Camp discipline could be gentle and almost humorous, tough, or even deadly. For minor infractions of camp rules, soldiers would be ordered to do extra guard duty, or march in hot sun or rain while they carried a heavy log instead of their rifle. Slightly more serious violations of military conduct would put a man inside an open barrel which he would have to "wear" with suspenders around camp. The barrel would carry a sign describing the offense: "Swearing," "Stealing," "Absent from Work." Still more serious offenses would find a soldier "bucked and gagged." A soldier bucked and gagged had a rag tied over his mouth, his legs were bound with a stick behind his knees, and his hands were bound under the stick in front of his shins. This bound, sitting position on the cold ground was very painful.

Some Northern and Southern officers also hung unruly recruits by their thumbs or even had men flogged with a whip. Alfred Bellard saw Federals suspended by their thumbs on orders from overly aggressive officers. "It was such officers," Bellard recalled, "who received a stray ball occasionally on the field of battle." Robert Hale Strong felt the same

This sketch was printed in Harper's Weekly *in June 1862, showing a soldier being punished for being "too fond of whiskey."*

way about such officers. "I have no doubt that many officers were killed by their own men."

The most severe military discipline was execution, an ugly military ceremony specifically designed to strike terror in the hearts of witnesses. Military executions were used rarely, but they did occur. During the last six months of the war, there were 245 convictions by military courts for desertion from Robert E. Lee's army. Seventy of the convicted soldiers were sentenced to die, but only 39 were actually executed. In the Union army, of 267 executions, 3 were for spying, 18 for rape, 72 for murder, and 141 were men who had deserted the army while in combat.

Military executions by firing squad were meant to show the largest number of men the consequences of serious offenses and the probable result of deserting. Entire regiments were assembled for the affair. The condemned soldier was paraded past his former campmates. Sometimes the condemned was driven to his execution on a wagon—riding seated on his own coffin. Often, his coffin would be used as the seat on which the condemned soldier would be shot by the firing squad. If the trembling firing squad did not successfully murder the condemned, an officer would finish the execution. Father William Corby had to give spiritual comfort to a condemned Union deserter and the priest described the pathetic scene:

> Eight or ten thousand troops were drawn in a hollow square, with one end of the square vacant. The condemned man was placed at that end. A squad of twelve men, with muskets loaded by one of the sergeants, came forward. According to rule, the sergeant puts no ball in one of the guns [just gunpowder], and no one knows whether his gun has a ball in it or not. The twelve soldiers, under the command of an officer, stood in front of the condemned man. The sentence was read and the provost-marshal drew a cap over the man's eyes. Then the officer gave the stern commands, "Get ready, aim, fire!" Eleven bullets struck the young man; still he was not dead. The provost-marshal was obliged to use his own revolver to put him out of pain.

After the execution, the watching regiments were marched past the dead man to cement in their minds what happens to deserters.

In November 1864, Confederate Colonel William Lamb witnessed a double execution of two deserters from the 36th North Carolina Artillery. One of the two condemned men did not die from the first round of bullets by the Rebel firing squad. Colonel Lamb remembered that "He groaned distressingly, 'Lord, have mercy on me,' when I immediately ordered up

Pickets from both sides would meet in friendship, exchange newspapers, coffee, and tobacco, and then return to the business of being enemies.

the reserve of four to within two paces of him and he received two shots through the head and died. . . . After the execution, the troops were broke up into columns and marched around the bodies."

Such scenes might have inspired the January 1863 letter home from Corporal James P. Coburn of the 141st Pennsylvania Volunteers: "I have concluded not to desert this week at least."

But the occasional execution for desertion, and bucking and gagging for being absent without permission did not stop the steady erosion of armies in both the North and South as weary, hungry men slipped away from cold, filthy camps. By February 1863, nearly one-fourth of the Union's Army of the Potomac was absent without leave. And by the time General Lee surrendered the Army of Northern Virginia in April 1865, at least 161,000 Confederates had simply wandered away from their threadbare and starving army. Throughout the war, the Federal desertion rate was about 10 percent and the Confederate rate was 14 percent.

Beyond the day-to-day tedium of camp life between battles, beyond the hunger and disease and the piles of dead friends, many men deserted their posts after receiving heartbreaking letters from home. They learned from the steady flow of mail that their wives, parents, and families could not survive or earn a living with their fighting men away from home year after year. Others laid down their weapons when fleeting moments of civility between blue and gray enemies suggested that both sides were really killing and maiming other Americans much like themselves.

Especially when opposing armies went into extended winter quarters, Union and Confederate forces were often only shouting distances apart. Blue and gray soldiers often mingled freely with their enemies no matter how much their officers tried to stop such "fraternization." When men could sneak out of their own lines and share peaceful words with their enemies, each tried to secure from the other what his own camp lacked. The men bartered between the lines, trading Yankee coffee for Rebel tobacco. Newspapers were also very popular in such trades. When long periods of quiet between opposing armies allowed, the commerce of trade would occur for weeks on end. Informal truces allowed the exchanges to continue without anyone getting hurt. Elisha Hunt Rhodes and his Rhode Islanders enjoyed such a truce in June 1863, just before blood flowed in torrents at Gettysburg: "[W]e are near Fredericksburg. Our regiment was immediately sent upon picket duty, way off to the left of our lines, and here we remained until morning without sleep. We arranged with the Rebels that neither side should fire unless an advance was made."

Confederate Lieutenant William R. Slaughter of the 6th Alabama Volunteers wrote a letter to his sister about the strange peace between the lines only two

And at the end, many brave men had fallen on the battlefield and were buried in graves in Pennsylvania, Virginia, Georgia, Mississippi . . .

days after the vicious battle of Fredericksburg on December 13, 1863: "The Yankees' line was about six hundred yards from ours, in full view, and our pickets were about 200 yards apart. Soon after light, they appeared with a flag of truce to collect their wounded between the picket lines which was granted. The pickets now laid down their guns and, meeting upon halfway ground, such another swapping of buttons, knives, pipes and giving salt and coffee for tobacco you never heard of."

But such fragile truces could not obscure the genuine hatred which inspired both sides to massacre each other for four years. In March 1862, Confederate T. W. Montfort wrote to his wife, "Teach my children to hate them with that bitter hatred that will never permit them to meet under any circumstances without seeking to destroy each other." And Confederate Sergeant Edwin Fay wrote home in July 1863, "I expect to murder every Yankee I ever meet when I can do so with impunity if I live a hundred years and peace is made in six months. Peace will never be made between me and any Yankee if I can kill him without too great risk."

★ ★ ★

Having started the war as eager recruits, having trained "Straw foot! Hay foot!" until they could march like real soldiers, having learned to live in dog tents and survive on "worm castles" and bad water, and having finally "seen the elephant," hardened veterans never stopped longing for home. Private Constantine Hege of the 48th North Carolina Volunteers wrote to his parents in December 1862: "I never knew how to value home until I came in the army."

. . . while others survived and marched home to the work of uniting a nation.

And when it was finally over, at least 360,000 Yankees and 258,000 Rebels were dead. Two-thirds of the Federals and three-fourths of the Confederates died from disease and not from wounds. In the North, one of every ten white men of military age was dead; in the South, one of every four white men of military age was dead.

Confederate John Childress was killed fighting for his country. The soldier's last words were recorded in the wartime diary of E. D. Patterson on August 31, 1863: "I am killed. Tell Ma and Pa goodbye for me." And his comrades and enemies who survived marched home to repair a devastated nation.

Glossary

bluecoats	Term used for soldiers in the Northern Union army during the Civil War because of the color of their uniforms.
Confederacy	The Confederate States of America; the South.
Confederate	Citizen of the Confederate States of America; a Southerner during the Civil War.
draft	Mandatory enlistment in military service.
drilling	Marching and training for military service.
Federals	A name used for members of the Union.
graycoats	Term used for soldiers in the Southern Confederate army during the Civil War because of the color of their uniforms.
hardtack	A rock-hard soda cracker issued as the main ration of food to many soldiers in the Civil War.
Rebels	Term used for Southerners in the Civil War.
reveille	A bugle call or drum roll to waken soldiers at sunrise for the first military formation of the day.
shebangs	Two-sided tents constructed of materials scrounged from the countryside around the camp.
tattoo	A call in the military to prepare for the end of the day.
Union	The United States of America; the North.
Yankees	Term used for Northerners during the Civil War.

Further Reading

Beatty, John. *The Citizen Soldier, or, Memoirs of a Volunteer*. Wilstach, Baldwin, Cincinnati, 1879.

Bellard, Alfred. *Gone for a Soldier: The Civil War Memoirs of Private Alfred Bellard*. David H. Donald, ed., Little, Brown, Boston, 1975.

Eisenschiml, Otto and Ralph Newman. *The Civil War, An American Iliad*. Mallard Press, New York, 1991.

Gragg, Rod. *The Illustrated Confederate Reader*. Harper and Row, New York, 1989.

Leckie, Robert. *None Died in Vain: The Saga of the American Civil War*. HarperCollins, New York, 1990.

McCarthy, Carlton. *Detailed Minutiae of Soldier Life*. McCarthy and Co, Richmond, 1882.

McMurry, Richard M. *Two Great Rebel Armies*. University of North Carolina Press, Chapel Hill, 1989.

McPherson, James M. *Battle Cry of Freedom*. Oxford University Press, New York, 1988.

Mitchell, Reid. *Civil War Soldiers*. Viking, New York, 1988.

Rhodes, Elisha Hunt. *All for the Union*. Robert Hunt Rhodes, ed., Orion Books, New York, 1985.

Robertson, James I., Jr. *Soldiers Blue and Gray*. University of North Carolina Press, Columbia, 1988.

Strong, Robert Hale. *A Yankee Private's Civil War*. Ashley Halsey, ed., Henry Regnery, Chicago, 1961.

Tapert, Annette. *The Brothers' War: Civil War Letters to their Loved Ones from the Blue and Gray*. Times Books, New York, 1988.

Wiley, Bell Irwin. *The Life of Johnny Reb: The Common Soldier of the Confederacy*. Bobbs- Merrill, Indianapolis, 1943.

_____. *The Life of Billy Yank: The Common Soldier of the Union*. Bobbs-Merrill, Indianapolis, 1952.

Williams, George F. Bullet and Shell: *War as the Soldier Saw It*. Fords, Howard and Hulbert, New York, 1882.

Websites About the Soldier's Life in the Civil War

Civil War Interactive, Food in the Civil War:
    http://www.almshouse.com/new_page_1.htm
Civil War Potpourri:
    http://civilwarhome.com/potpourr.htm
The United States Civil War Center:
    http://www.cwc.lsu.edu/

Index

Index

Photo Credits

Harper's Weekly: pp. 13, 14, 17, 18, 21, 23, 54, 56; Library of Congress: pp. 10, 25, 28, 30, 31, 34, 36, 42, 48, 52, 58, 59; United States Army Military History Institute: pp. 20, 29, 32, 39, 44 (top), 44 (bottom), 47